Times and Rhymes

Verses from the life of my Great Grandfather

By John Moon

Copyright © 2018 by John Moon. All rights reserved.
ISBN-13: 978-0-692-11176-5

Foreword

It is my sincere hope that this small book will be worthy of my great grandfather's approval. But I also hope that a few other people might find some of it's contents enjoyable.

Whether it be to family or friends (often even everyday letters he wrote in rhyme and verse. Two to four pages long.) or verses expressing great joy, love, or deep sadness, he wrote what was in his heart.

My great grandparents Herbert and Cornelia might be called Civil War baby boomers as they were both born in 1866. Herbert's father Clark was a sergeant in the Union Army. Cornelia's parents were married a few days before Lee's surrender to Grant at Appomattox. Some of her mother's aunts and uncles were abolitionists and conductors on the Underground Railway.

Both Herbert and Cornie's pedigrees in America stretch back to sixteen thirties Massachusetts Bay Colony, Maine, and New York. Cornie had three ancestors who fought for America during the Revolutionary War. My ongoing journey to piece together my genealogy and artifacts along with my desire to understand my ancestral relations continues to be a life altering experience.

If even one person now or in the future is touched by Great Grandfather Herbert then surely he would smile on this effort.

Let us test that last verse of "Times and Rhymes", shall we?

Times and Rhymes

I have written some rhymes.
In my short spare times.
I have found in life, as the years go rolling on.
    And no one tells.
From where they come, or where they've gone.
    My idle spells,
        These odd spare times.

    Since I have begun,
My time has onward passed;
    Some I have written
        To my friends dear
And many I've penned to loved ones at home.
    To many these rhymes
I've written in my short spare times
    May be joyful chimes
And songs of pleasure to some
        That will even sing
        And chime and ring
When I have at last gone home
    And life is done.
                      HES

For One and For All

When the daylight brightness fades into the west,
And the tired old sun has sunk to it's rest,
'Tis then that the cool evening shadows fall.
      Over one and over all.

When the little stars put forth their feeble light,
Doing their part to light up the night,
And the silvery moon comes over mountains tall
      To shine over one and all.

Then the hum of the tiny cricket is heard,
And other insects and sometimes a bird.
Will go winging its way to some tree top tall.
      Merrily singing for one and for all.

The old earth is resting from it's busy day,
And the quiet of night starts to hold its sway.
I'm longing and wishing to issue a call
      Not just to one but for all.

To come, and share my pleasures, though small.
While away the moments and let's forget all,
Our sorrows and sadness however great,
      And not let them trouble us again once
            and for all.

Herbert:-
In future years when turning to sway
The social joys of many a happy day.
If on these lines you chance to cast
Your eye recalling scenes of pleasure
Long gone by. Pause as you read
And briefly lend a tranquil
Recollection of a friend.

Your Friend
Carrie Lathrop

Irving Park Jan 20th 1882.

Thoughts

There are thoughts, that are dear.
There are thoughts, that give cheer.
    There are thoughts, that are sublime.
There are thoughts, that we all cherish.
There are thoughts, that never perish.
    There are thoughts, not worth a dime.
There are thoughts, that are beautiful.
There are thoughts, of the dutiful
    There are thoughts, we cannot forget
There are thoughts of the needy.
There are thoughts of the care free.
    There are thoughts no one would forfeit.
There are thoughts of the weary and the sad.
There are thoughts of the cheery and the glad.
    There are thoughts of the loving and the kind.
There are thoughts of the thinking of all mankind.
                                     HE Stover

Faith

Faith that endureth to the end,
    Will have it's reward in time.
Hold steadfast to your belief,
Then you'll never come to grief.

Hope

Hope abounds within the breast,
    And entertained by many a man.
Those who can hope and hope aright
    Their future prospects will be bright.

Charity

Charity when the needy call,
    Should be ever kind to all.
And in all things should be kind,
    And ever extended to all mankind.

Endeavor

We have our beginnings,
                in little things.
We always commence,
                at the start.
We struggle and fight for
                the greater things
And attain if we do
                not lose heart
We struggle through life,
                with might and main.
We plan and plan,
                for our success.
Some of us are able to,
                endure the strain.
But many are unable to
                endure the stress.
We're always looking forward,
                for rewards.
We strive and toil
                with this in view.
When the big things come
                to us-wards
We feel that we've won,
                what was due.
Then let us struggle on in,
                this busy life.
And not stumble or fall
                neath our load.
For success is sure to
                reward the strife.
When we come to the end
                of the road.

                              HE Stover

A worthless woman! more cold clay.
As all false things are! but so fair
She takes the breath of men away
Who gaze upon her. So beware.

C F Matteson

Oak Park Ills
March 30/84

Enchantment

Distance they say, lends enchantment to the view.
I surely would like this enchantment to behold.
For you are my enchantment true.
No other enchantment will just quite do.

I am enchanted by your very style.
I've seen no other quite so captivating.
I am enchanted by your winning smile.
Really to me, it is just the thing.

Your enchantment is so inspiring.
It buoys me to the highest pitch.
I sing your praises without tiring.
To have such enchantment really makes me rich.

Enchantment O' Enchantment.
You seem so far removed from me just now.
But before long I'm quite confident,
My enchantment will return to me, somehow.
H.E.S.

Office of The Metropolitan Business College
Nos. 77 AND 79 MADISON ST.
OPP. McVICKERS THEATRE
G. L. HOWE
O. M. POWERS, Proprietors

Chicago, April 26, 1884.

This certifies that Herbert Hoover has attended our school one year and pursued the business course. He has a good record while in school, both as to study and conduct, and we cheerfully recommend him to the confidence of anyone desiring the services of an exemplary, industrious and honest young man.

Respectfully,
Howe & Powers

Waste Not

Waste not the time that you have here.
    Time is fleeting on hurried wing.
Too soon opportunities will disappear.
    Then too late 'twill be to do the thing.

Grasp the moments ere they fly.
    Use them for the best results.
You will not regret the try.
    When it's life's evening and your sun sets.

Now is the time to improve your plans.
    Be wise and alert to your chance.
Improve your methods and plans.
    Then there'll be naught to enhance.

Use each swiftly fleeting minute.
    If you'd accomplish your aim
Make sure of your object. Get into it.
    If not you have yourself to blame.

Time is now yours to use.
    And now is your chance to try.
Chances will pass. Then not abuse
    Your time. Improve those moments, ere they fly.
                      HES

To-day is Life

What is life? Just a day.
    Born at morn, then swept away,
By time. Those fleeting hours,
    For a short time only, were ours.

Yesterday came and went the way,
    Of every yesterday. Gone to stay.
They never come back, no not one.
    For each day bringeth a new sun.

To-morrows are always yet to come.
    They never reach us. No not one.
We know not what they have in store.
    For they've never been here before.

Now, the day that's here is to-day.
    Not to-morrow nor yesterday.
This is the day we live, and the time.
    For we live only a day at a time.

Then let us make the best of to-day.
    Not count much upon the results of yesterday
Nor in to-morrow put our trust.
    But do to-day the thing we must.
                  HES

May Blessings attend you
Both early & late
May heaven defend you
In choosing you mate

Carrie. E. Matteson
Oak Park

Never the Same

I shall never be the same,
Since into my life you came.
    Nothing around me seems to be quite right.
For whenever you are near;
There's plenty of life and cheer.
    I cannot bear to have you from my sight.

I shall never be the same.
All my efforts seem so tame.
    You have cast o'er me a spell so dense.
I can scarcely see ahead.
All else seems to be dead.
    For the memory of you holds me in a trance

I shall never be the same,
In sunshine or in rain.
    All I can see is a lovely vision of you.
My heart is no longer mine;
Since I've exchanged it for thine.
    I feel so different since I met up with you.
                        H.E.S.

Yesterday

My yesterdays that have so swiftly gone
Were full of joy and lith with song.

My to-morrows, O' what will they be?
If hopes and wishes will but come true

I'll be sure of pleasures and happiness too
In the to-morrows that's sure to be.

Books are a treasure
We all should hoard.
    They are the best friend of man.
They are full of riches,
And should be stored
    Whenever and wherever we can.

Love is not Blind

They say Love is blind.
    I'm not so sure, this is true.
For if Love as they say,
Is so very blind;
    How in the world, could I have ever found you?

Love is not blind.
    Love does not grope around in the dark.
For if Love as they say,
Is so very blind;
    How do you suppose it gives out Love's spark?

They say Love is blind.
I'm quite certain, it looks into the heart
For if Love as they say,
Is so very blind;
    How could I have singled you out from the start?

Love is not blind.
    Now it could not possibly be.
For if Love as they say,
Is so very blind;
    How in the world, could you have ever found me?

H.E.S.

Ah sad, sad fate

When it early got late

And the time for our parting came

When good bye we did say

With longing for the day

When we could meet again.

You'll be coming round the mountain.
    At the setting of the sun.
'Tis then I'll do some shouting
      When to your home you come.
                HE Stover

Since Into My Life You Came

I've altered all my plans.
I've changed my mind completely.
    I used to see things in a haze,
    But now for me dawns brighter days.
    Even the birds seem to sing more sweetly,
        Since into my life you came.

All the universe seems changed.
The stars give out a brighter glow;
    As they twinkle far up in the azure blue.
    I used to think all my joys were through;
    But, now I know it cannot be so,
        Since into my life you came.

The flowers have put on a brighter glow.
The trees and grass a fresher green.
    Even little rivulets seem bubbling over,
    As they gently glide through fields of clover.
    Life for me has become more serene,
        Since into my life you came.

A lucky day it was for me,
When fate threw us to-gather.
    I changed all my views of life;
    Which to me had seemed so full of strife,
    Now all is sunshine, no matter what the weather,
        Since into my life you came.

When You Are Near

When you are near,
Life for me is full of cheer.
Never a day is dull and drear.
When you are near.

When you are near
There's naught but sunshine to be had.
The very twinkle in your eye makes me glad.
When you are near.

When you are near,
And your merry smile I see
Nothing else really matters to me.
When you are near.

When you are near.
With your ever beguiling charm
I have no cause to take alarm.
When you are near.

When you are near
There's no need of any other
Why should I seek any farther.
When you are near.

When you are near,
You are all I could desire
There is naught else I require.
When you are near.

HES

Clarence Elmer Stover

C arry your chin high old boy.
L et not mere troubles you annoy.
A lways look up and never down.
R emember he who sinks will surely drown.
E very time that you feel that your down.
N ever flinch or cast a frown, but
C heer up and try it out once again.
E very effort is a step toward a gain.

E ach and every effort you make
L eads to success in what you undertake.
M ind and memory are good things to have.
E ach of them you need in order to thrive.
R are opportunities may come to you yet.

S hould you endure and not forget
T o grasp them as they come your way.
O n every occasion, trust in the Lord.
V erily He is your only God.
E ver be cheerful and with your lot be content
R emember 'tis from Him, all things to you are sent.

              Your bro Herb.

To a Daughter

My little girl sweet
So trim and so neat.
How I have loved you these many days.
Through all care and strife,
You've been the joy of my life;
With your cute and cunning ways.

You have been to me,
What no other could be;
No matter how hard they should try.
For in you I have found
All that's good, true and sound.
You are the apple of my eye.

HES

A Wish

I wish for you every joy of life.
    I wish for you health and strength
I wish for you friends old and new;
    Who will ever be honest and true.

I wish that happiness be yours without end,
    And from sorrows and trials you'll always be free;
That all that is noble and grand
    Will ever and ever abide with thee.

I wish you success in every venture.
    And not a failure in any plan you make;
Or that you'll have cause for regret,
    And never, never make the mistake;

Of forgetting the one whose wishes true
Were always meant only, just for you.

        HES

Bliss

When stillness of the night,
                     Begging to fall,
And through the lowering glim
                     The coo coos call.
When each little star comes a peeping out
                     One by one,
And the evening zephyrs whisper
                     Good bye to the sun,
Day is done. And home the weary
                     Come to rest.
Freed at last from the dreary tasks
                     Like birds to nest.
The noise and tumult of the day
                     All are stilled.
His cup of joy and happiness
                     Seems well filled.
At home with his loved ones
                     All about.
Stilled the din of the day and
                     It's noisy shout.
Sweet silent, beautiful night.
                     O, what bliss.
Can anything be likened
                     Unto this.

Regret

The sun is fading in the west.
    I've tried this day to do my best.
I may have failed some things to do,
    But the Master knows I didn't intend to.

If this day I injured one.
    Or from my duties I have run.
I beg another chance be mine.
    I'll not so careless be next time.
                        HE Stover

Regret

I'm sorry I can't be with you to-day,
And look into your face, and be able to say
Congratulations my little girl to you.
Just to let you know, daddy is still thinking of you.

Cheer Up

Just what shall I say,
Upon this bright cheerful day
    That will cheer you up a bit?
While the bright sun is shining
There should be no repining
    Or no sorrow or sadness to mar it.

Flowers in great profusion everywhere.
Brilliant birds are flitting here and there
    The whole world seems so bright and gay.
Soft zephyrs are skimming o'er the ocean blue.
Skies are shimmering in the self same hue.
    Now what else is there for me to say?

God giveth to us those beautiful flowers,
And also He giveth the freshening showers.
    That they might be blessings to you and I.
Let's grasp each and every shining moment, then
Breathe a thoughtful prayer now, and then.
    We'll have no cause for a tear or sigh

Joyous laughter and merriment
Are truly from our maker sent
    To each of His creatures here below.
Then let us join with the happy throng,
And keep in His sunshine all day long.
    For upon us His love He doth bestow.

Great Days

In the days long, long ago
    When childhood was full of joy
I played and romped the whole day through
    With nothing to fear or annoy.

I rambled here and gamboled there
    And played in many a game,
Not giving life a thought or a care.
    Life to me was only a game.

Joy and happiness without an end.
    Had all I wanted and more,
Nothing to give or nothing to spend.
    From all that I had in store.

Energy, strength and daring huge.
    Never a thought of the morrow.
No worry, no strife not even a grudge.
    And no sighing, sadness or sorrow,

Great days they were, and many.
    Then as happy as a lark.
Even though I had not a penny
    From daybreak until dark.

Grand days they were, without ban.
    Hopes and desires bright and gay
Wonderful ideas as to the man
That I should grow to be some day.

        HE Stover

Sunday

The toils of the week
              Are at an end.
And to the meeting house,
              Our way we wend.
To worship him.
              Who gave his life
That we might rest
              From care and strife.
To sing the songs
              That praise his name.
To read his word
              And be sure and gain.
Remittance from all sins
              And errors quite
If we are steadfast
              And live right.
Sunday that blessed day
              When toll the glad bells.
That gladden all hearts.
              And to each spirit tells,
Of the Just and Holy One
              Who set aside this day,
And bode all to come
              And worship who may.
                      HE Stover

Backgammon

Backgammon's the game
For you and a dame.
You just roll out the dice.
You're in luck.
If you hit the buck.
With doubles, which are nice.

Sometimes it's a four,
Sometimes it's more.
You never know just what you get.
When in a fix.
You hit a six
Then you're going some, you bet.

When in a tight place.
You flop a brace.
And can move four men at a time.
You're in great luck.
To get out of the muck.
And get all those men in a line.

Mr. and Mrs. Clarence E. Stover
announce the marriage of their daughter
Ramona Adelphine
to
Mr. Norris J. Reasoner
on Friday, May twenty-eighth
nineteen hundred and twenty
Eugene, Oregon

At home
after June twenty-first
at Christian Church
Deming, New Mexico

Backgammon (continued)

Another roll.
You take the toll.
An ace, and a duce, O heck!
Why could I not,
Get a whole lot,
So I could move more than a speck.

Then you get rough.
And with a huff
You remove one of my men from the board.
Then with a quake,
I take a shake.
To see if I can have my man restored.

Thus we wend
Toward the end.
We shake until our arms are lame.
First you hit,
Then I hit,
A double and so ends the game.

HES

Some of These Days

Some of these days,
    We'll be merry and gay.
Some of these days,
We'll know how to pray.

Some of these days,
    Fairer skies will be ours.
Some of these days,
    For there'll be no more showers.

Some of these days,
    We'll have ceased to fight.
Some of these days,
    We'll know what is right.

Some of these days,
    When? Who can tell.
Some of these days,
    We'll bid the world farewell.

Some of these days,
    Our cares will be through.
Some of these days,
    For me and for you.

        HE Stover

To My Daughter Who Married

Dear little girl of mine.
   Dear little sweetheart of mine.
You were the light of my day.
With that sweet smile of thine,
That abode with me all the time.
   I miss you now that you are gone away.

Dear little girl of mine.
Dear little sweetheart of mine.
   The echo of your voice ever haunts me;

And I very much miss
Your dear loving kiss
   Now that you've gone away.

Dear little girl of mine.
Dear little sweetheart of mine.
   The days full of darkness be,
And sorrow fills my heart,
Now that we are apart.
   Knowing that you've gone to stay.

                    Your loving Daddy
                          H E Stover

I wish for you better joys to come.
I wish much happiness and plenty of luck
Continued good health, I'm wishing for you.
And I'm wishing that my wishes will all come true

Good health- Good luck-Good times- Good friends.
And everything good that fortune sends.
May these be yours and give you cheer
On this your birthday,
And throughout the whole year.

Eva Kryger

E ver fair and always sweet.
V ery chic and O! so neat.
A lways trim from head to feet.

K eeping pace with the very best.
R anging sweetness that will stand the test.
Y ou are surely a lovely being. that
G oes from me with much feeling
E ach and every day. Your kind is
R eally very hard to find.

      Your Daddy
       HE Stover

To My Grandson Robert
Play the Game

Play the game. Run the race.
And in all things keep the pace.

Play the game. Reach the goal.
If you falter you pay the toll.

Play the game for the game's sake.
Play it fair much is at stake.

Play the game with all your might.
And as you play it be sure you're right.

Always remember a well-played game
Rewards many with a well-earned name.

Play the game for all that is in it.
Play the game square and you'll win it.

Roy Carlton Moon

R ip-snorting about most every sport.
O f any and most every sort.
Y our delight is to angle for fish.

C annot stand to eat of this dish, but
A s fortunate as many as regards to luck.
R iding around in that old laundry truck.
L ike to tipple a little now and then
T he same as many other men.
O n the cigarette question you take the cake
N ever mind the brand, any suits first rate.

M eals you are always looking for
O f certain diets from the store.
O n some occasions you sleep too much.
N ever caring much for any lunch

HES

To my other half
Mother Cornie

Believe it or not.
    There's nothing I've got.
That I would not share with you.
Be it money or food.
    There's nothing too good
That you should not have some of it too.

If it's merely a smile.
    Tis not worth the while.
Unless you have a share in it too.
Why should I laugh.
    If you do not have half.
Useless; unless you are in it too.

Even in my dreams.
    To me it seems.
That you should be a part of them too .
And when I think.
    There's always a link.
That binds you into it too.

So wherever I go
    I want you to know.
That whatever is good and true.
You are mine.
    For all time.
And the best that I have is for you.
                           HE Stover

Dorothy Glarson

D oing the things you like to do,
O r down in the dumps and oft' times blue.
R aving about your terrible lot;
O r wishing for things that you have not.
T hinking out ways to have some fun.
H oping every minute you'll have some.
Y earning for things beyond your grip.

G etting yourself into a terrible fit.
L etting your best chances go by.
A lways building castles in the sky.
R aring to go most anywhere.
S ighing and fretting wherever you are,
O r worrying over the things that are not
N ever satisfied with what you've got

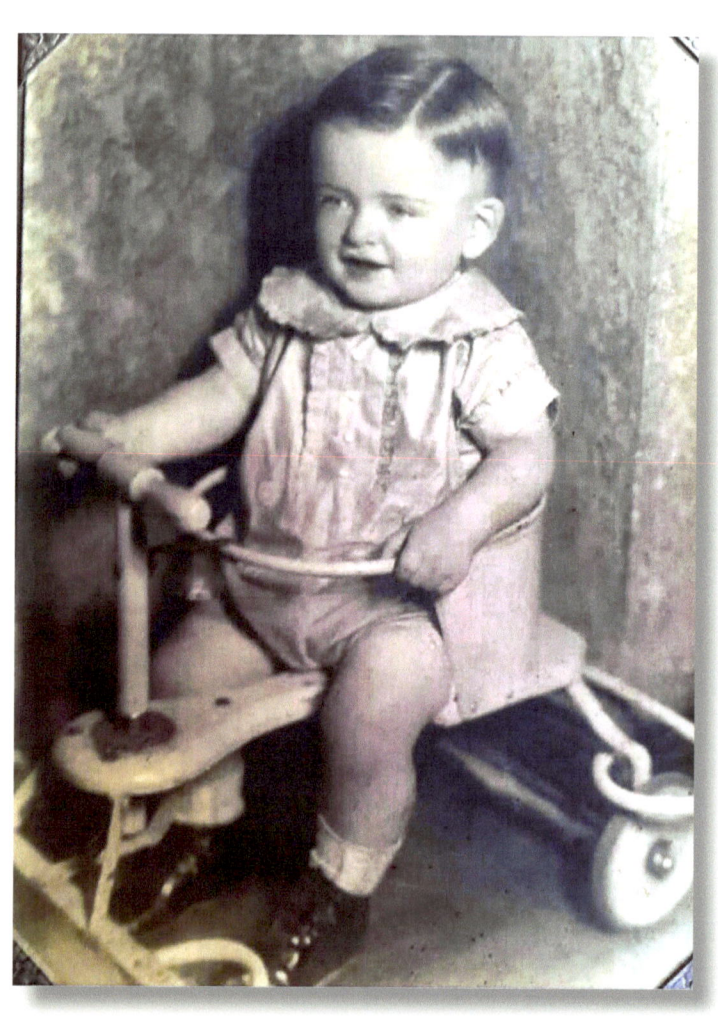

Roland

I want you to know, while I'm still here
That naught else to me, was ever so dear;
As your baby form, and face like a flower
That, smiling and cooing hour by hour
Twined tendrils of love so fast round my heart
No distance, nor time can break them apart.

Blossom of youth turns to fruitage of years,
Helps confidence take the place of my fears.
Dawn of young manhood rests on your brow
See that I'm proud of you always, as now.
Right living and thinking, the best of life,
The goodwill of others is worth the strife.

I've lived my life over in you, my Dear.
Pray you don't cause me a pang or tear.
You are the first and the last in my mind.
No pearl of great price like thee, shall I find.
In childhood, in youth, and in after years.
Remember my smiles, and forget my tears.

Herbert E. Stover

The Old and The New

Another year has drawn to a close.
Let it pass with all it's woes.
There were bitter times in 1932.
With many heart aches, and many were blue.

Now a new one has come to take it's place
And with it new hopes to all our race.
For better times in this 1933 year.
And trust 'twill bring to all more cheer.

Yes the old year has gone at last.
Let's forget the errors that have past.
And as the new one dawns again,
Let our new page be without stain.

Let's make good promises and true.
And let our thoughts be always pure.
Keeping all good resolutions made.
And our actions free from all shade.

Open and above board everything.
Ready to catch the peace bird on the wing.
Nothing hidden that should be seen.
And our backs turned to all that's mean.

Happy New Year, may it be so.
To every creature on earth below.
                              HE Stover

June 12 1933

Fiftieth Anniversary of the Royal League
    A Fraternal Order of which I have been
a member for 39 years.

Royal League.
        Grand old name.
        You've earned every right to fame.

These Fifty Years.
        You've stood every test,
        And now your rated among the best.
Those Many years.
        You've held your head high,
        Allowing none other to pass you by.

Those Golden years.
        And in all the realm,
        You've had grand men at your helm.

(Continues on next page)

(Continued from last page)

Those Fifty years,
> You've paid up all claims
> Yet plenty of surplus still remains.

Those Wonderful years,
> We have backed every plan
> And stood shoulder to shoulder, every man.

Those Trying years,
> Our boys have stood by,
> With willing hands and effort to try.

> Herbert Stover
> Past Archon and
> First Collector at
> Jefferson Council
> # 118 Royal League

Memories

For forty odd years, I had a companion true.
I knew not what it was like to be alonesome then.
We were so happy, and considerate, too;
But time changed all these things for me when

The Master reached out His hand and said,
" Come, dwell with me, thou tired one "
" Come, rest upon my breast, thy weary head. "
" For unto you I say, beloved, well done. "
She left me, went into the great beyond.
That is why I am so lonesome now.
But sweet memories of her still abound,
And they serve to comfort me, somehow.

STOVER—Cornelia Matilda Stover, at 932 Marco place, Venice. Beloved wife of Herbert Stover, and mother of Mrs. Myrtle F. Moon.

1933

Funeral services Friday, July 7th, at 2 p. m., at the Ocean Park parlors of Kirkelie, Bernard & Peek. Interment Inglewood Park cemetery.

I've Seen

In my walks of earthly life
I've seen much of care and strife.
I've seen the shades and shadows fall.
I've seen the darkness of the pall.

I've seen the dawn of early morn.
And with it new hopes were borne.
Then with the hot noon days sun
Those hopes fade out one by one

Then I've seen the evening chill,
Settle down, o'er vale and hill.
Then come the darkness of the night.
And drown those precious hopes from sight.

I've seen youth stealthily depart,
And all it's pleasures leave the heart.
Then the advance of stern manhood.
Here in youths place hath stood.

At last grey age, a creeping, come.
Sneaking along, then hide the sun,
Of all life's bright, shining light.
Then deluge all into darkest night.

HE Stover

Sept. 1934
Robert Carlton Moon
Age 13

R ight now is your time, to prepare for college.
O n every occasion, you should improve your knowledge.
B e faithful and true to every endeavor.
E xacting the truth from all without favor.
R each out for the best things in this life.
T reat each of your fellows without any strife.

C arefully guard your every word.
A lways practice your anger to curb.
R ather be poor than be dishonest.
L iving a life that is only the best
T hinking of others once in a while.
O bliging and courteous with a smile.
N ever ceasing to do the worthwhile.

M ay your way through life be on the square.
O ffering your needy fellow man, of your sustenance a share.
O ccupy your time for the best results, and
N ever, O never offer any insults.

Grandpa Stover

Patients And Patience

Up among the shrubs and flowers;
In neat little bungalows so trim,
Lie many patients for hours and hours.
    Some so wan and some so thin,
    And the weather sometimes so very hot.
    One feels like melting on the spot.

Patients they are, you may be sure;
For patience they must have to endure,
All their physical troubles so long.
    Just waiting till time shall make them strong.
    As they will then their health regain.
    And be able to mingle with the world again.

The nurses must be patient too;
For to be otherwise would not do.
Their toils and trials are so many.
    Of praise they get little if any.
    They must care for all these patients well;
    For without proper patience, who can tell,
    What gross mischief might be done.
    To these patients, every one.

God's blessings then be upon all of you.
Patients and patient nurses too.
    While you lie there for hours and hours;
    Up among the shrubs and flowers.

                        HE Stover

Sept. 1934

To Mrs. Gillespie at Olive View Sanitorium
Who has a butterfly tattoo on her knee

A cute little butterfly,
    As pretty as could be;
Went searching for some honey,
    And paused upon her knee.

She tried with all her might and main,
    To shoo the little fellow away.
But the more she shooed, the butterfly booed
    Not on your life, I'm here to stay.

He'll get his fill of honey, I'm sure,
    While he's perched upon that mound;
For unto this very time and day,
    Little butterfly still sits around.

              H.E. Stover

Myrtle Frances Moon

M ay your health return to you.
Y our friends be ever kind and true.
R eal pleasures always with you abound.
T hat you will gain weight pound by pound.
L ittle by little you're sure to improve.
E ach and every day you do not move.

F ull of pep and ginger too.
R aring to go that is you.
A s happy and gay as any.
N ever mind the dead gone past.
C heer up and forget all that's past.
E ver look forward then you'll thrive.
S mile and be glad that you're alive.

M y very best hopes are all of you.
O ! surely you'll come smiling through.
O nce you adhere to nature's way.
N ever again need you be that way.

                                        HE Stover

Sept. 1934
Roland Francis Moon
Age 5

R ougish little fellow that you are.
O ur little mischief and mimic star.
L aughing at any and most every thing.
A lways trying your best to sing.
N ever caring much about how things go.
D aring and boisterous, and great for show.

F ull of frolic and fancy free.
R ough as they make them, as one can see.
A lways a happy go lucky kid.
N ever a worry about anything much.
C arefree and luckier than most of the bunch.
I know you're the boy of your daddy's heart.
S triving to imitate him in every part.

M aking a din and racket is your bent.
O therwise you would not quite be content.
O! Surely you're just all boy.
N othing less than your mother's joy.

Grandpa Stover

Dec. 18-34
A Birthday Wish For Myrtle

Here's
Wishing your birthday might happier be.
Please accept this little gift from me.
Hoping that it will help to brighten your natal day.
And trust that the next one will be more gay .

I'll not forget that day little lass;
When you blessed our home, long ago past;
With those great big eyes of azure blue.
I could see heavenly sunlight a shining through.

With that chubby little face so round and bright,
And those little hands that clung so to mine .
To me, they were such a blessed sight.
O! boy, was I a proud daddy? and feeling fine.

Old father time has such a way
Of changing things from day to day.
Altering our faces and our forms;
As we go battling life's storms.

I've only one regret, I'm sorry to say.
Why could we have not kept you unto this day.
That sweet little bundle of joy untold,
Why! o why? did you have to grow old?

Your Loving Father

Just The Odd One

As I travel the world all alone
Not a mate I can call my own
      'Tis often I pause and with a moan.
I long for a companion who would be true.
One who is faithful, it could be you.
      But alas I'm just the odd one.

Where I go folks seem to be in pairs.
Joy and happiness seem to be theirs.
      While I struggle on all alone.
No one with which my joys to share.
No one who seems to give me a care.
      For I'm just only an odd one.

Just the odd one, wherever I go.
Just the odd one, without any show
      Of being united with anyone.
Just floating along like a wind blown leaf.
Here and there, my stay is but brief.
      Since I'm just the odd one.

                    HES

Some Things

Some of our hopes,
     'Tis sad to say,
     Are sure to be blasted;
     From day to day.

Some of our wishes,
     Although of the best;
     May not come true,
     When it comes to a test.

Some of our longings,
     However sincere;
     Will never be known,
     Though we shed a tear.

Some of our thoughts,
     However so good;
     Are best left unsaid,
     They might not be understood.

(Continues on second page)

Some Things (Continued)

Some of our memories,
    We'll cherish them ever;
    Others will fade,
    And be gone forever.

Some of our ideals,
    So grand and fine,
    Are liable to be gnashed,
    At most anytime.

Some of our sorrows,
    Though grievous they are;
    Are best kept secluded,
    Lest others happiness they mar.

Some of our days,
    Will be happy and gay;
    Some will be gloomy and sad,
    Life has ever been that way.

                                                      H. E. S.

A Longing For A Friend

When the darkness of the night doth creep,
And the tired old sun has sunk to it's rest;
Then I long for the nearness of a friend like you.
Who would wish for me, only the best.

When the stars twinkle in the azure blue,
And the silvery moon is shining bright.
I love to sit in my old rocking chair
And dream only of you, in the dim twilight.

As I peer up into the vaulted blue
I often wonder if it can ever be;
That you will always be to me, a friend good and true.
And some sweet day, you'll return to me.

When the evening zephyrs cool,
My heated brow doth press.
Memories of you always console me;
And I seem to feel your loving caress.

In my waking hours, I miss you much.
In my slumbers, I dream only of you.
Perhaps, you will never know of my deep longing,
And perhaps you will never care, although I was true.
Some day somewhere, some time.
I feel that our paths will cross again
And then I trust, my very dear friend,
That you will be near me, to remain.

HE Stover

Lonesome

As life's evening twilight draws near.
And my pathway seems so dark and drear.
    With only memories of yesterdays in mind,
All alone by myself without a soul to cheer
I long for the associates that in the past I have held dear.
    Or the helpful hand of some friend. I find
That my wishes and longings are all quite in vain
For I cannot recall those dear associates again;
    As many of them have passed into the beyond
I alone am lingering here just for a spell
Awaiting the call, then to bid farewell,
    To the world, and sever life's bond.
HES

Dread

When the early morning sunlight
Casts its beams across my bed.
I awaken from my fitful slumbers,
With a sinking kind of dread.

For I know the day will drag so drearily along.
With so little or nothing much that I can do.
Unable like others to mingle with the throng.
Always obliged to forgo the things I like to do.

With dark forebodings and dreaded fears.
Just sitting around with only my thoughts;
And wishing I were not so along in years.
Longing for the health that I have naught.

A friend or so, who would be true;
Or perhaps a kindly neighbor would not hurt;
Or if I was able to take pick and shovel,
And go out in the garden and dig in the dirt.

Might some of my monotony relieve;
And would aid to make my days much brighter.
Then I would more contented be.
For my cares and worries would be some lighter.

I always long for the shades of night
To fall, when all shall be still and calm.
For the darkness then, would shut out all the lights.
Then I would lie down to rest, with sleep for balm.

HES

Childhood Days

I am thinking to day.
    Of that land far away.
Where first I saw the light of day.
Of the trees and the brooks
And the still quiet nooks
    Where the bees and the birds want to play.

Where the river ran clear.
    Through the meadows quite near
And the old farmhouse white.
Wherein all was delight.
    Surrounded by tumbledown fence.

Tall warming corn in the fields nigh.
Beneath the warm summer sky.
    And the roses about the door.
Give forth their odors sweet.
And the blue violets trim and neat.
    I would never ask for more.

Gone are those bright happy days.
Lost in the mist and haze.
    Of the years that have swiftly passed.
How oft I have pondered
And oft I have wondered
    Why those precious days did not last.

        Continues on next page

Continued from previous page

Time with swift wings,
Changed all those things.
    And left me just memories dear,
Of the glad times I had;
With dear Mother and Dad
    And not a want or a fear.

All this has gone and past.
Too simple, too lovely to last.
    The ones I loved, I see no more.
Faith in the land of the blest
Leaves the hope within my breast.
    That I shall again, meet those I adore.

                    HE Stover

A Thought

Perhaps, when I have left this world behind.
People may wish they'd been less unkind,
And been more thoughtful of the one, who
Was always willing to see them through.

                    HE Stover

Old Age

Youth has gone.
        Age is here.
The song has fled.
        The outlook drear.
All laughter passed.
        Could not last.
Life fast fleeting.
        Soon be over.
Hope sustaining.
        And more sober.
        Faith much greater.
        For what comes later.
Love is strong
        As was ever.
Sure to continue,
        And cease never.
        But grow at length,
        To full strength.
Steps more faltering,
        Growing more weak.
Desires less great.
        Thoughts more meek.
        Wishes more true,
        And naught to rue.

        Continued on next page

Continued from previous page

Health declining.
    Sight more dim.
Hearing weakened.
    Nearing the rim,
       Of the other shore.
Where we part again no more.
HES

Days

Days come and days go.
A little older each day we grow.
Life keep moving silently along.
Soon 'twill be just another song.
Yes he was here and now he's gone
The way of all the mighty throng.

We got many thrills
A roaming them thar hills,
Gathering sweet flowers here and there.
Those were the happy days,
When we had easy ways.
And our skies were never more fair.

STOVER. Late of 7622 South Hobart. Herbert E. Stover, aged 70 years.
Services Friday at 2:30 p.m. at E. B. McCormick's Funeral Home, 4601 Crenshaw Boulevard. Interment, Inglewood Park Cemetery.

Photos / Descriptions

Cover photo-- Ladies watch purchased in 1874 by Great Grandmother Cornelias' Grandmother Ann

2. Great Grandfather Herberts' father Clark Stover, 1st Wisconsin, 3 mos., 33rd Wisconsin Company I, 3 yrs.
4. The same watch in cover photo.
6. Herbert 1884
8. 10. 12. 14. Entries from Herberts' autograph book. 10 is by his penmanship teacher at Metropolitan Business College, Chicago IL.
16. Recommendation from Metropolitan Business College.
18. Herbert.
20. Entry from Herberts' autograph book
22. Herbert was a member of the Sons of Illinois Veterans of the Civil War.
24. Great Grandmother Cornelia 1884.
26. Cornelia 1884.
28. Ladies watch Herbert gave Cornelia in 1892. The year before they were married.
30. Tin type of Herbert and Cornelia from 1893. The same year they were married.
32. Herberts' brother Clarence {Cad), sister-in-law Jess, and their daughter Ramona. 1898.
34. My Grandmother Myrtle. Three years old. 1899
36. Myrtle. September 1904.
38. Standing in rear, Clarence and Jess. Seated left to right: Ramona, Cornelia's mother Frances, Ramona, Cornelia's father Junius. San Fernando, CA. 1906.
40. Herbert.

42. Grandmother Myrtle, sixteen years old. Graduation picture.
44. and 46. Sketches by Herbert.
48. Herbert and Cornelia were members of this church.
50. Ramona. 1917.
52. Wedding invitation.
54 Clark's funeral at First Congregational Church, Chicago, Illinois, One of the the church's founders was Philo Carpenter. Brother of Cornie's grandmother
56. My Grandparenfs (Roy and Myrtle) wedding picture. 1918.
58. My Grandmother (Myrtle).
60. My Grandmother's sister Eva and her husband Frank .
62. My Uncle Bob. 1924.
64 My Grandfather Roy holding my father. 1928.
66. Great Grandmother Cornelia.
68. Standing from left to right. Frank Glarson's sister {name unknown), Dorothy Glarson, Frank Kryger, Eva, Herbert and Cornelia. Seated in front. Uncle Bob, Frank Glarson holding his son, and my Grandfather Roy holding my father. Thanksgiving 1929.
70. My father.
72. Napkin ring.
74. Past Archon medal awarded to Herbert in 1899.
76. Reverse side of medal on page 7 4. ·
78. Herbert and Cornie's last picture together August 1932.
80. Cornelia's death notice.
82. Uncle Bob on the left. My father on the right.
84. and 86. Olive View Sanitorium. My Grandmother Myrtle contracted tuberculosis and would have been required to go there for treatment. She was there in1934.

88. Great Grandfather Herbert on the left. Grandmother Myrtle in the middle and Grandfather Roy on the right.
90. My father. September 1934.
92. Myrtle.
94. 96.Herbert.
98. Sketch by Herbert in Cornelia's autograph book. Probably 1891.
100. 102. 104. Sketches by Herbert.
106. Herbert's mother Martha.
108. As far as I know, the last picture taken of Great Grandfather Herbert.
116. The reverse side of watch on front cover.

Appendix

Time & Rhymes

I have written some rhymes
In my short spare times
I have penned at times, as the years go rolling on,
    And as one fills
Forever here they come, where they're gone.
    My idle times,
    Those odd spare times.

    Since I have begun,
My time has onward passed;
    Some I have written
    To my friends dear
And many I've penned to loved ones at home.
    Is mostly these rhymes
I've written in my short spare times
    May do some good sometime
And bring pleasure to some
    That will ever sing
    And shine and ring
When I am at last safe home
    And life is o'er.
                                        Revised
                                          J.E.J.

The One of For All.

When the day light brightness fades in the West,
And the tired old sun has sank to its rest,
'Tis then that the cool evening shadows fall.
    Over one and over all.

When the little stars put forth their feeble light
Doing their part to light up the night
And the silvery moon comes o'er mountains tall
    To shine over one and over all.

There the hum of the tiny cricket is heard,
And other insects and sometimes a bird.
Will go winging its way to some tree top tall,
    Merrily singing for one and for all.

The old earth is resting now its busy day,
And the quiet of night starts to hold its sway,
I'm longing and wishing to issue a call
    To all, just one and for all.

To come, share my pleasures, though small.
While away the moments and let's forget all,
Our sorrows and sadness however great,
    And not let them trouble us again ever
        and for all.

This year is swiftly drawing to a close.
And where we'll be next nobody knows.
Yet I have much faith, and some hope too.
That all will be well with me and you.

And now that I've said all that I can
I'll close this epistle the way I began
Love to Brother Cad and Sister Jess.
And that's about all for this time I guess.
    Your versified Bro
      Hert

X   Thoughts.

There are thoughts, that are dear.
There are thoughts, that give cheer.
 There are thoughts, that are sublime.
There are thoughts, that we all cherish.
There are thoughts, that never perish.
 There are thoughts, worth a dime.
There are thoughts, that are beautiful.
There are thoughts, of the dutiful.
 There are thoughts, we cannot forget.
There are thoughts of the needy.
There are thoughts of the care free.
 There are thoughts no one would profit
There are thoughts of the weary and the sad.
There are thoughts of the cheery and the glad.
 There are thoughts of the loving and the kind.
There are thoughts of the thinking of all mankind.

78 To my Grand Son Robert.

Play The Game.

✝ Play the game, Run the race,
And in all things keep the pace.

Play the game, Reach the goal,
If you falter, you pay the toll.

Play the game for the game's sake,
Play it fair. Much is at stake.

Play the game with all your might,
And as you play it. Be sure you're right

Always remember a well played game.
Rewards many with a well earned name.

Play the game or all that's in it
Play the game square, and you'll win it.

— Faith. —

✝ Faith that endureth to the end.
Will have its reward in time.

Endeavor

We have our beginnings,
          in little things.
We always commence,
          at the start.
We struggle and fight for,
          the greater things.
And attain them if we do
          not lose heart.

We struggle through life,
          with might and main.
We plow and plan,
          for our success.
Some of us are able to,
          endure the strain.
But many are unable,
          to stand the stress.
We're always looking forward,
          for rewards.
We strive and toil with
          this in view.
When the big things come,
          to us-wards.
We feel that we have won,
          what was due.
Then let us struggle on in,
          this busy life.
And not stumble or fall
          'neath our load.
For success is sure to,
          reward the strife.
When we come to the end
          of the road.

                    H. E. Jones

Enchantment

Distance they say, lends enchantment to the view.
 I surely would like this enchantment to behold.
For you are my enchantment true.
 No other enchantment, will just quite do.

I am enchanted by your very style.
 I've seen no other quite so captivating.
I am enchanted by your winning smile.
 Really to me it is just the thing.

Your enchantment is so inspiring.
 It buoys me up to the highest pitch.
I sing your praises without tiring.
 More such enchantment makes me rich.

Enchantment O' Enchantment.
You sure so far removed from me just now.
 But before long I'm quite confident,
 My enchantment will return to me, somehow.
            L.E.J.

You'll be coming round the mountain.
 At the setting of the sun.
Tis then I'll do some shouting,
 When to your house you come.
            L.E.Jones

Waste not

Waste not the time that you have here.
Time is fleeting on hurried wing.
To soon Oppertunities will disappear
Then it's to late 'twill be to do the thing.

Grasp the moments ere they fly.
Use them for the best results.
You will not regret the try.
When it's life's evening, and sun sets.

Now is the time to improve your plan
Be wise and do it to your advantage
Improve your methods and your plan
Then there'll be naught to —

Use each swiftly fleeting minute
If you'd accomplish your aim
Make sure of your object —
If not you have left yourself —

Time is now yours to use
And now is your chance to try.
Chances will pass. Then do not lose
Your time. Improve these moments ere —

Then sove them up
And keep from the rut
   That so many often fall in.
Then save them to-day
Now while you may.
   To squander is really a sin.

                                 H.E. Stiver

          To-day is Life.
What is life? Just a day.
   Born at morn, then swept away,
By time. Those fleeting hours,
   For a short while only, were ours.

Yesterday came and went the way,
   Of every yesterday. Gone to stay.
They never came back, no not one.
   For each day bringeth a new sun.

To-morrows are always yet to come.
   They never reach us. No not one.
We know not what they have in store.
   For they've never been here before.

Nay, the day that's here is to-day.
   Not to-morrow nor yesterday.
This is the day we live, and the time
   For we live only a day at a time.

Then let us make the best of to-day.
   Not count much upon the results of yesterday
Nor in to-morrow put our trust.
   But do to-day the thing we must.
                             H.E. Stiver

Never the Same.

I shall never be the same;
Since into my life you came.
  Nothing around me seems to be quite right.
For wherever you are near,
There's plenty of life and cheer.
  I cannot bear to have you from my sight.

I shall never be the same.
All my efforts seem so tame.
  You have cast o'er me a spell so dense.
I can scarcely see ahead.
All else seems to be dead,
  For the memory of you holds me in a trance.

I shall never be the same,
In sunshine or rain.
  All I can see is a lovely vision of you.
My heart is no longer mine,
Since I've exchanged it for thine.
  I feel so different since I met up with you.

H.E.F.

Olive View Sanitarium

The Sanitarium out at Olive View,
Is a very good place for not just a few.
  It wishes best to the very many,
Asking little of some, from others not any.
Funds which are so always needed,
  That the health of its patients may be speeded.

H.E.F.

And now I must stop,
And let you know where to drop;
   A line or two if you will.
Or should you come with a boy
You will find me and how,
   At 1941 S. Sycamore Ave. near the hill.

If you find the time
Remember old Sunshine
   And come out sometime and see him.
I never hesitate I am about
You'll find my latch string out.
   Give it a pull and just walk in.

                    Old Man Sunshine
                         H. E. Jean

X Ah, sad, sad fate
   When it early got late;
      And the time for our parting came.
   When good-byes we did say,
   With longing for the day.
      When we could meet again.

Since into My Life you Came

I've altered all my plans.
I've changed my mind completly.
   I used to see things in a haze;
   But now for me dawns brighter days.
   Even the birds seem to sing more sweetly,
        Since into my life you came.

All the universe seems changed.
The stars give out a brighter glow,
   As they twinkle far up in the azure blue.
   I used to think all my joys were through.
   But now I know that it cannot be so.
        Since into my life you came.

The flowers have put on brighter hues.
The trees and grass a fresher green.
   Even little rivulets seem bubbling over,
   As they gently glide through fields of clover.
   Life for me has become more serene.
        Since into my life you came.

A lucky day it was for me,
When fate threw us so happily together.
   I changed all my views of life;
   Which to me seemed so full of strife.
   Now all is sunshine, no matter what the weather.
        Since into my life, you came.

When you are near.

When you are near,
Life for me is full of cheer;
Else a day is dull and drear,
When you are near.

When you are near,
There's naught but sunshine to be had.
The very twinkle in your eye makes me glad.
When you are near.

When you are near,
And your merry smile I see
Nothing else really matters to me.
When you are near.

When you are near,
With your ever beguiling charm,
I have no cause to take alarm.
When you are near.

When you are near,
There's no need of any other,
Why should I seek any father.
When you are near.

When you are near,
You are all I could desire,
There is naught else I require.
When you are near.

H.E.J.

Clarence Elmer Stover

Carry your chin high old boy.
Let not mere troubles you annoy.
Always look up and never down.
Remember he who sinks will surely drown.
Every time that you feel that your down.
Never flinch or cast a frown, but
Chuck up and try it out once again.
Every effort is a step toward a gain.

Each and every effort you make
Leads to success in what you undertake
Mind and memory are good things to have
Each of them you need in order to thrive
Rare opportunities may come to you yet.

Should you endure and not forget.
Tagrasp them as they come your way.
On every occasion, trust in the Lord
Verily He is your only God.
Ever be cheerful and with your lot be content
Remember tis from Him, all things to you are sent.

Your Bro Herb.

Thus we inning
Toward the end.
We shake till our arms are lame;
First you hit,
Then I hit.
A double and so ends the game.

                                                H.E.J.

To a Daughter.

My little girl sweet,
Trim and so neat.
How I have loved you these many days.
Through all care and strife,
You've been the joy of my life;
With your cute and cunning ways.

You have been to me,
What no other could be;
No matter how hard they should try.
For in you I have found
All that's good, true and sound.
You are the apple of my eye.

                                                  H.E.J.

Now if you don't like this verse.
Don't let me hear you curse.
Instead chuck it all into your fire.
Forget all you've read.
Acannot she said.
My lines dident make the flames go higher.
　　　　　　　　　　H.E.S.

　　　　　　I Wish

X　I wish for you every joy of life.
　　I wish for you health and strength.
　I wish for you, friends old and new,
　　to be with ever be honest and true to you.

　I wish that happiness be yours without end,
　　and your troubles and totals you will always
　That all of it be noble and grand,
　　　　　　ever abide with thee.

　I wish you success in every venture,
　　And not a finance in any plan you make,
　So that you'll ever have cause for regret.
　　　　　　never make the mistake;

　To everyone the one who's wishes true,
　　who's always meant only just for you.
　　　　　　　　　　H.E.J.

Regret

X The sun is fading in the west.
   I've tried this day to do my best.
I may have failed some things to do.
   But the Master knows I didn't intend too.

If this day I've injured one.
   Or from my duties I have run.
I beg another chance be mine.
   I'll not so careless be next time.
                                    H E Town

Bliss

X When stillness of night,
                begins to fall.
And through the lowering gloom.
                The Coo coo's call.
When each little star comes a peeping;
                one by one
And the evening zephirs whisper
                Good by to the sun.

Day is done; and home the weary,
                comes to rest.
Tired at last from the dreary tasks
                like birds to nest.
The noise and the tumult of the day.
                all are stilled.
His cup of joy and happiness
                seems well filled.
At home with his loved ones
                all about.
Stilled the din of the day and
                its noisy shout.
Sweet, silent, beautiful night.

Can anything be likened,
                unto this

Regret

X The sun is fading in the west.
  I've tried this day to do my best.
  I may have failed some things to do.
  But the Master knows I didn't intend to.

  If this day I've injured one.
  Or from my duties I have run.
  I beg another chance be mine.
  I'll not so careless be next time.
              —H. E. Twin

Bliss

X When stillness of night,
                begins to fall.
  And through the lowering gloom
                The Cuckoo's call.
  When each little star comes a peeping,
                one by one
  And the evening zephers whisper
                Good-by to the sun.

  Day is done; and home the weary,
                comes to rest.
  Tired at last from the dreary tasks
                like birds to nest.
  The noise and the tumult of the day.
                all are stilled.
  His cup of joy and happiness
                seems well filled.
  At home with his loved ones
                all about.
  Stilled the din of the day and
                its noisy shout.
  Sweet, silent, beautiful night

  Can anything be likened,
                unto this

Myrtle Frances Moon.

May your health return to you.
Your friends be ever kind & true.
Real pleasures always with you abound. &
That you will gain weight pound by pound.
Little by little you'r sure to improve.
Each and every day you do not move.

Full of pep and ginger too.
Raring to go, that is you.
As happy a day as any.
Never mind the dead gone past.
Cheer up and Forget all that's past.
Ever look forward, then you'll thrive.
S mile and be glad that you'r alive.

My very best hopes are all for you.
O surely you'll come smiling through.
Once you adhere to natures way.
Never again, need you be that way.
H. E. J.

Regret

I'm sorry I cannot be with you to-day
And look into your face and be able to say.
Congratulations my little girl to you
Just to let you know, daddy is still thinking of
you.

Cheer Up.

Just up to say I say,
Upon this bright happy day;
  That you'll cheer yourself up a bit,
While the bright sun is shining;
There should be no repining;
  Or no sorrow or sadness to mar it.

Flowers are in great profusion everywhere.
Brilliant birds are flitting here and there.
  The whole world, seems to be so bright and gay
Soft zephyrs are skimming o'er the ocean blue.
Skys are shimmering in the self same hue.
  Now what else is there for me to say.

God giveth those beautiful flowers,
And also the freshening showers.
  That they might be blessings to you and I.
So grasp each and every skipping moment, then
Breathe a thankful prayer now, and then
  We'll have no need for a tear or sigh.

Joyous laughter and Merriment,
Are truly from our Maker sent;
  To each of his creatures here below.
Then join with all the happy throng.
And keep in his sunshine all day long.
  For He doeth upon us his love bestow.

Great Days

In the days, long, long ago.
    When childhood was full of joy.
I played and romped the whole day through,
    With nothing to fear or annoy.

I rambeled here and gambeled there.
    And played in many a game.
Not giving life a thought or a care.
    Life to me then was only a game.

Joy and happiness without an end,
    Had all I wanted and more.
Nothing to give or nothing to spend,
    From all that I had in store

Energy, strength and dareing huge.
    Never a thought of the morrow.
No worry, no strife not even a grudge.
    And no sighing, sadness or sorrow,

Great days they were and many
    Thru as happy as a lark,
E'en though I hadden't a penny.
    From day break until the dark,

Grand days they were, without care.
    Hopes and desires, bright and gay

Sunday.

The toils of the week
    Are at an end.
And to the meeting house,
    Our way we wend.
To worship him
    Who gave his life.
That we might rest
    From care and strife.

To sing the songs
    That praise his name.
To read his word
    And be sure and gain.
Remittance from all sins
    And errors quite
If we are steadfast
    And live aright.

Sunday that blessed day
    When toll the glad bells.
That gladden all hearts.
    And to each spirit tells,
Of the Just and Holy One
    Who set asside this day,
And bade all to come
    And worship who may.

                  H. Finn

Backgammon

Backgammon's the game.
For gyves and a dame.
You just roll out the dice.
You's in luck.
If you hit the buck.
With doubles which are nice.

Sometimes it's four.
Sometimes it's more.
You never know what you'll get.
When in a jis.
You hit a six
Then you'r going some you bet.

When in a tight place.
You flop a brace.
And can move four men at a time.
You'r in great luck.
To get out of the muck.
And get all those men into line.

Another roll.
You take toll.
An ace, and a duce. O luck!
Why could I not.
Get a whole lot.
So that I could move more than a speck.

Then you get rough.
An' with a huff
You remove one of my men from the board
Then with a quake,
I take a shake.
To see if I cannot have my man restored

Some of these Days.

Some of these days,
  Will be merry & gay.
Some of these days,
  Will know how to pray.

Some of these days,
  Fairer skys will be ours.
Some of these days,
  For there'll be no more showers.

Some of these days,
  Will have ceased to fight.
Some of these days,
  Will know what is right.

Some of these days,
  When? who can tell.
Some of these days,
  We'll bid the world farewell.

Some of these days,
  Our cares will be through.
Some of these days,
  For me and for you.

H. E. Stover

104   Little Forgotten

To my Daughter
    Who Married.

✗
Dear little girl of mine.
Dear little sweetheart of mine
   You were the light of my day.
With that sweet smile of thine,
That abode with me all the time.
   I miss, now that you've gone away.

Dear little girl of mine.
Dear sweetheart of mine.
   The echo of your voice ever haunts me;
And I very much miss
Your dear loving kiss
   Now that you've gone away.

Dear little girl of mine.
Dear little sweetheart of mine.
   The days full of darkness be,
And sorrow fills my heart,
Now that we are apart.
   Knowing that you've gone to stay.

                    Your loving Daddy
                         H. H. Moss

162   Sept 1934

To Mrs Gillespi at Olive View Sanitarium
who has a butterfly tatooed on her knee.

A cute little butterfly,
   As pretty as could be;
Went searching for some honey,
   And paused upon her knee.

She tried with all her mite & main,
   To shoo the little fellow away.
But the more she shooed, the butterfly cooed
   Not on your life. I'm here to stay.

He'll get his fill of honey, I'm sure,
   While he's perched upon that mound;
For unto this very time & day.
   Little butterfly still sticks around.

                       H. E. Stover.

— · —

      Eva Stryger.

Ever fair & always sweet.
Very chick & Oh so neat.
Always trim from head to feet.

Keeping pace with the very best.

78   To my Grand Son Robert.

Play the Game.

† Play the game. Run the race.
And in all things keep the pace.

Play the game. Reach the goal.
If you falter, you pay the toll.

Play the game for the game's sake.
Play it fair. Much is at stake.

Play the game with all your might.
And as you play it. Be sure you're right.

Always remember a well played game.
Rewards many with a well earned name.

Play the game as all that's in it.
Play the game square and you'll win it.

— Faith. —

† Faith that endureth to the end.
Will have its reward in time.

166

By Carlton Moow.

Rip-snorting about most every sport.
Of any and most every sort.
Your delight is to angle for fish.

I am not stoned to eat of this dish, but
As fortunate as many as regards to luck
Riding around in that old laundry truck.
Like to tipple a little now and then
The same as many other men.
On the cigarette question you take the cake.
Never mind the brandy, any suits first rate.

Meals you are always looking for
Of certain diets from the store.
On some occasions you sleep too much.
Never caring much for any lunch.

H.E.J.

To my other half.

Mother Lovie

Believe it or not.
   There's nothing I've got.
That I would not share it with you.
Be it money or food.
   There's nothing to good.
That you should not have some of it too.

If it's merely a smile.
   'Tis not worth the while.
Unless you have a share in it too.
Why should I laugh.
   If you do not have half.
Useless; unless you are in it too.

Even in my dreams.
   To me it seems.
That you should be a part of them too.
And
   There's always a hint.
That binds you into it too.

So wherever I go
   I want you to know.
That whatever is good and true.
You are mine.
   'Tis all thine.
And the best that I have is for you.

Some of our days,
 Will be happy & gay;
 Some will be gloomy & sad,
 Life has ever been that way.
                              H.E.S.

           Dorothy Gearson.

Doing the things you like to do;
Or down in the dumps & of't times blue.
Raving about your terrible lot;
Or wishing for things that you have not.
Thinking but ways to have some fun.
Hoping every minute you'll have some.
Yearning for things beyond your grip

Getting yourself into a terrible fit.
Letting your best chances go by.
Always building castles in the sky.
Raring to go most any where.
Sighing & fretting where ever you are.
Or worrying over the things that are not.
Never satisfied with what you've got.

The Old and The New

Another year has drawn to a close,
Let it pass with all it's woes.
There were bitter times in 1932
With many heartaches, and many were blue.

Now a new one has come to take it's place,
And with it new hopes to all our race.
For better times in this 1933 year,
And trust 'twill bring to all more cheer.

Yes the old year has gone at last,
Let's forget the errors that have past.
And as the new one dawns again,
Let our new page be without stain.

Let's make good promises and true,
And let our thoughts be always pure.
Keeping all good resolutions made,
And our actions free from all shade.

Open and above board everything,
Ready to catch the peace bird on the wing.
Nothing hidden that should be seen,
With our back turned to all that's mean.

Happy New Year, may it be so,
To every creature on earth below.

J. E. Over

June 12 - 1933

Fiftieth Anniversary of The Royal League.
A Fraternal Order of which I have been
a member for 39 years.

Royal League.
 Grand old name,
 You've earned every right to Fame.

These Fifty Years.
 You've stood every test,
 And now your rated among the best.

Those Many years.
 You've held your head high,
 Allowing none other to pass you by.

Those Golden years.
 And in all the realm,
 You've had grand men at your helm.

Those Fifty years,
 You've paid up all claims,
 Yet plenty of surplus still remains.

Those Wonderful years,
 Men have backed every plan
 And stood shoulder to shoulder, every man.

Those Trying years,
 Our boys have stood by,
 With willing hands and effort to try.

 Herbert E. Farr,
 Past Archon &
 First Councilor of
 Jefferson Council
 #118 Royal League

I've seen.

In my walks of earthly life
I've seen much of care and strife.
I've seen the shades and shaddows fall
I've seen the darkness of the pall.

I've seen the dawn of early morn.
And with it new hopes were borne.
Then with the hot noon-days sun
Those hopes fade out one by one

Then I've seen the evening chill,
Settle down, over vale and hill.
Then came the darkness of the night.
And drown those precious hopes from sight.

I've seen youth stealthily depart,
And all its pleasures leave the heart.
Then the advance of stern manhood,
Here, in youths place hath stood.

At last grey age, a creeping come.
Sneaking along, then hide the sun,
Of all life's, bright, shining light.
Then diluge all into darkest night.

A. E. Steen

Sept 1934

Robert Carlton Moon

Age 13.

Right now is your time, to prepair for caledge.
On every occasion, you should improve your Knowledge.
Be faithful and true to every endeavor.
Exacting the truth from all without favor.
Reach out for the best things in this life.
Treat each of your fellows, with out any strife.

Carefully guard your every word.
Always practice your anger to curb.
Rather be poor than be dishonest
Living a life that is only the best.
Thinking of others once in a while.
Obligeing & courteous with a smile.
Never ceasing to do the worth while.

May your way through life be on the square.
Offering your needy fellowman, of your sustenance a share
Occupy your time for the best results, and
Never, O' never offer any insults.

Grandpa Steen

Patients & Patience

Up among the shrubs & flowers;
In neat little bungalows so trim,
Lie many patients for hours & hours.
   Some so warm and some so thin
   And the weather sometimes so very hot,
   One feels like melting on the spot.

Patients they are you may be sure;
For patience they must have to endure;
All their physical troubles so long.
   Just waiting till time shall make them strong.
   As they will then their health regain
   And be able to mingle with the world again.

The nurses must be patient too.
For to be otherwise would not do.
Their toils & trials are so many
   Of praise they get little, if any
   They must care for all those patients well.
   For with out proper patience who can tell,
   What gross mischief might be done.
   To these patients every one.

God's blessings then be upon all of you.
Patients & patient nurses too.
   While you lie there for hours & hours.
   Up among the shrubs and flowers.
                                    T. E. Stover

162   Sept 1934

To Mrs Gillespi at Olive View Sanitarium
who had a butterfly tatooed on her knee.

A cute little butterfly,
   As pretty as could be;
Went searching for some honey,
   And paused upon her knee.

She tried with all her mite & main,
   To shoo the little fellow away.
But the more she shooed, the butterfly booed
   Not on your life, I'm here to stay.

He'll get his fill of honey, I'm sure,
   While he's perched upon that mound;
For unto this very time & day.
   Little butterfly still sticks around.

                        H. E. Steer

— · —

           Eva Kryger.

Ever fair & always sweet.
Very chick & So neat.
Always trim from head to feet.

Keeping pace with the very best.
Possible a nature that will stand the test.

Myrtle Frances Moon.

M ay your health return to you.
Y our friends be ever kind & true.
R eal pleasures always with you abound. &
T hat you will gain weight pound by pound.
L ittle by little you'r sure to improve.
E ach & every day you do not rove.

F ull of pep & ginger too.
R aring to go, that is you.
A s happy & gay as any.
N ever mind the dead gone past.
C hear up & forget all that's past.
E ver look forward, then you'll thrive.
S mile & be glad that you'r alive.

M y very best hopes are all for you.
O ! surely you'll come smiling through.
O nce you adhere to natures way.
N ever again, need you be that way.

H.E.J.

Regret

I'm sorry I cannot be with you to-day
And look into your face and be able to say.
Congratulations my little girl to you
Just to let you know, daddy is still thinking of
you.

Sept 1934 **161**

Roland Francis Moon

Age 5

Roguish little fellow, that you are.
Our little mischief, and mimic star.
Laughing at any/and most every thing.
Always trying your best to sing.
Never caring much about how things go.
Daring and boisterous, and great for show.

Full of frolic and fancy free.
Rough as they make them, as one can see.
Always a happy go lucky kid.
Never a worry about any thing much
Care free and luckier than most of the bunch.
I know you're the boy of your daddys heart.
Striveing to imitate him in every part.

Makeing a din and racket is your bent.
Otherwise you would not quite be content.
O! surely you're just all boy.
Nothing less than your mothers joy.

Grandpa Stover

You are sure a lovely being. that
Goes from me with much feeling
Each and every day. Your kind, is
Really very hard to find.

Your Daddy
M. Stover

Myrtle Frances Moon.

May your health return to you.
Your friends be ever kind & true.
Real pleasures always with you abound. And
That you will gain weight pound by pound.
Little by little you'r sure to improve.
Each and every day you do not move.

Full of pep and ginger too.
Raring to go, that is you.
As happy and gay as any.
Never mind the dead gone past.
Cheer up & Forget all that's past.
Ever look forward, then you'll thrive.
Smile and be glad that you'r alive.

My very best hopes are all for you.
O! surely you'll come smiling through.
Once you adhere to nature's way,
Never again, need you be that way.

H.E.J.

Regret

I'm sorry I cannot be with you to-day
And look into your face and be able to say.
Congratulations my little girl to you
Just to let you know, daddy is still thinking of
you.

168
Just The Odd One

As I travel this world all about
For a mate that I can call my own
 I often pause, and with a moan
I long for a companion, who would be true.
One who would be faithful, it could be you —
 But alas I am just the odd one.

Where I go folks seem to be in pairs
Joy and happiness seem to be theirs
 Still I struggle on all alone.
No one with which my joys to share.
No one who seems to give me a care.
 For I'm only just the odd one.

Just the odd one, wherever I go
Just the odd one, without any show.
 Of being united with any one
Just floating along, like a wind blown leaf
Here and there, my stay is only brief.
 Since I'm just the odd one

N.E.J.

Some Things

X

Some of our hopes,
   'Tis sad to say;
   Are sure to be blasted;
   From day to day.

Some of our wishes,
   Although of the best;
   May never come true,
   When it comes to a test.

Some of our longings,
   However's sincere;
   Will never be known,
   Though we shed a tear.

Some of our thoughts,
   However so good;
   Are best left unsaid,
   They might not be understood.

Some of our memories,
   We'll cherish them ever;
   Others will fade,
   And be gone forever.

Some of our ideals,
   So grand & fine;
   Are liable to be quashed,
   At most any time.

Some of our sorrows,
   Though grievous they are;
   Are best kept secluded,
   Lest other's happiness they mar

Longing for a Friend

When darkness of the night doth creep,
And the sun has sank to its rest.
Then I long for the nearness of a friend like you.
Who will only wish for me, the very best.

When the stars twinkle in the azure blue,
And the silvery moon shines so bright.
I love to sit in my old rocking chair
And dream only of you in the dim twilight.

As I peer up into the vaulted blue.
I often wonder if it can ever be;
That you will ever be to me a friend good and true.
And that some sweet day you'll return to me.

When the evening zephers cool,
My heated brow doth press.
Memories of you always console me;
And I seem to feel your loving caress.

In my waking hours, I miss you much.
In my slumbers, I dream only of you.
Perhaps you will never know of my deep longing,
And perhaps you will not care; although I was true.

Some day, somewhere, some time.
I feel that our paths will cross again.
And then I trust, my very dear friend,
That you will be near me to remain.

H. E. Glenn

Dread.

When the early morning sunlight,
    Casts its beams across my bed.
I awaken from my fitful slumbers,
    With a sinking kind of dread.

For I know the day will drag so drearily along.
    With so little or nothing much I can do.
Unable like others to mingle with the throng.
    Always obliged to forego the things I'd like to do.

Having dark forebodings of dreaded fears.
    Just sitting around with just my thoughts;
And wishing, I were not so along in years.
    Longing for the health, that I have naught.

A friend or so who would be true;
    Or perhaps a kindly neighbor would not hurt
Or if I was able, to take pick and shovel.
    And go out in the garden and dig in the dirt.

Might some of my monotony relieve,
    And would aid to make my days much brighter.
Then I would more contented be.
    For my cares & worries would be some lighter.

I always long for the shades of night.
    To fall, when all shall be still and calm.
For the darkness then would shut out all the light.
    Then I could lie down to rest, with sleep for balm.

                                      A.E.J.

All the blooms are past,
Temple, too lovely to last.
Them one I build, I see no more.
With in the bounds of the Best.
Leaves the hope within my breast.
That I shall again meet those I adore.
                                    H. E. Stover

Old Age.

X Youth has gone.
    Age is here.
The song has fled.
    The outlook drear.
    All laughter passed.
    Could not last.
Life just fleeting
    Soon be over.
Life sustaining
    And more sober.
    Faith much greater,
    For what comes later.
Love is strong
    As was ever.
Hope continues,
    And cease never.
    But grows at length,
    Till full strength.
Steps more tottering,
    Growing more weak.
Duties more great.
    Though more meek.
    ...
    And ought to rest.
Death is nearing.
    Light more dim.
Hearing weakened
    Meaning the sum,
Of the other shore
    When we shall no ...

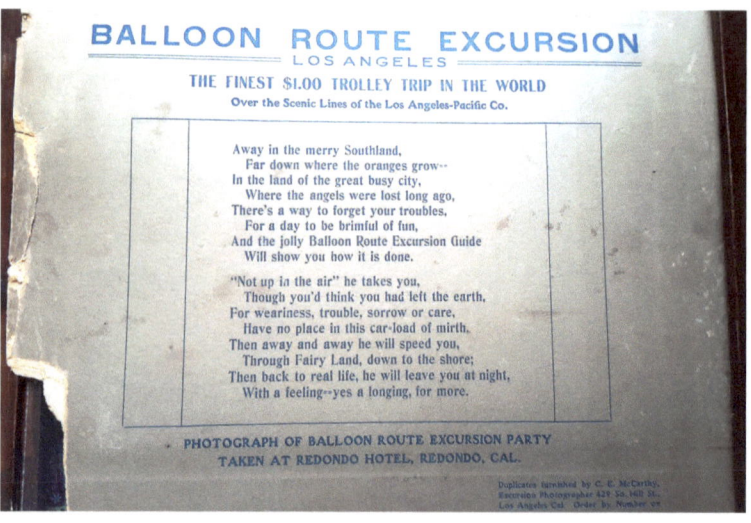

www.ingramcontent.com/pod-product-compliance
Lightning Source LLC
Chambersburg PA
CBHW041629220426
43665CB00001B/3